Fortress

Jim Bennett

Poems 6

Fortress

Poetry is about truth, yet this is a work of fiction in that names and places of characters are used purely for convenience. Any resemblance to actual persons, living or dead, events, or locales, is entirely accidental.

Cover Image and Design by Rory d'Eon
Visit deon.ca to find Rory and his products and services!
Original (atrocious) photographs by Jim Bennett

Published by **Lulu (Paperback)**
ISBN **978-1-927900-01-7**

Acknowledgements

I owe a debt of gratitude to everyone who ever criticized or challenged me, including those whose encouragement in the dark times kept me going.

My writers' group deserves special mention for their unabashed opening of my eye when it was blind to missed possibilities or possible misinterpretations.

A special thanks to Cathy Miyata and Tony Sims for proofreading, and critiquing, the first draft. Their input caused a re-think of a number of decisions - wordings, inclusions, exclusions.

I should mention Inge. H. Borg and Joseph Spuckler, whose recent encouragement helped me 'get back to the table' and put this collection together.

I should mention the many, many Kindle Book Review authors who have entrusted this curmudgeon with their works and endured his parsing of their literary children. It's been a lot of time and effort for all of us, and definitely worth it. There's nothing like seeing writing rather unlike one's own to make one think there are other ways of thinking.

I owe a lifelong debt to Richard Ketchum, who gave me permission to be weird and different, and to write from whatever point of view I found myself in. Richard made me believe that I can do this.

I hope that my reviews of others have at least occasionally been encouraging for them. They deserve it.

Finally I must thank my wife Pat, whose longsuffering includes putting up with a weird curmudgeon who spends inordinate amounts of time at a keyboard, when not mousing spider solitaire. A prerequisite to creativity is a stable platform. A woodworker has a table and tools, but needs the lights to stay on. Patty makes the world light up on time. An artist in her own right, and a formidable sewing/craftsperson, she has patience and insight. I merely grumble and scribble.

I have a website, www.jim-bennett.ca where you can find my earlier books, my blog, and references to other writers and helpers.

Table of Contents

Table of Contents (cont.)

Table of Contents (cont.)

Possession

I sat to rest in the back yard

and dozing
I was home again
not this last place but another
after my father died
it was not my grass even while mowing
the rosebush disliked me
and I could not name any flowers
except for forget-me pansies
but at night one summer
maybe their dog but no rude watchers
grumbling how much food cost
or how lucky I was for shelter
lying sleeping-bag naked to priceless stars
that yard became mine
and its dark shapes talked to me
it was not time yet for leaving dreams
now I wake in a plastic chair past sunset
and hear this other surrounding space
whisper in comfort
come to rest with me
and this still waiting precious silence
will be yours

Wakeup Call

bad dream:
I'm fast at work
longing for vacation -

wide walks, good talks, smiles together -

not this

Second Look

better
in hindsight, much
nicer than promised, past
life together: watch our children,
grow old

Shadows

Fireflies
flirt past twilight:
my loneliness flickers
remembering love sparked in such
darkness

Résumé

we live

caricatures

of what we once would be:

mere animated outlines of

real dreams

Peeper

sweet tight
bikini, tops
fetching matching bottom
can't *imagine* what she looks like
naked

Stag Star

high heels
and not much else
she opened her address:

(we watched her opening a dress)

"high, heels"

Music Night

since you ask me,
these jazz musicians
play like sex, close and personal,
unlike your stolid violinists
who masturbated their instruments
with pizzicato at the frog
in concert-ed postures
while cymbals clashed and French horns blared,
a breathlessness conducted to a score

but in the next night club inhalation
you make soft suggestions
that raise intentional questions:
would I dally for esthetics,
think overture can reach improvisation,
am I out of tempo due to ethics,
or pausing to time the next smooth riff
to add to your counterpoint
toward closing movement

this is more like jazz, where nothing's written down
uncertain of next second's implications
we are sharing a cab to somewhere;
will the new moon watch our full accompaniment
or night go dark when we reach your door
now kissing your upturned face
while taxi speeds away afraid to witness
your unlocking, scripted or extempore
climax

Tour, Song

She's from Lisbon: imagine
her figure in fresh translation
as it sways to the tune a of a personal love
swinging sings sublime rhyme suggests sweet copulation
bridging lyrics regretful
rough words turn away leave unpleasant duets
unfinished
once requited, twice exploited
her sex lost now, but her body begins again
in its liquid foreign language
a tango beat begets mysteries of lust
straining postures of wanting
while she belts out Portuguese to a mostly Spanish
wine-warmed and overstuffed audience
until a tour group guide yells "Bravo",
someone chuckles "O Lay",
and the ale-faced UK tourists
to make their universe hold still
commence clapping in English

Condom Conundrum

or
Contraceptive Conception

"pro choice"
quoth amateurs:

when found out, they're "knocked up".

Real Girls who work Hard Streets insist:
Pro=Choice.

Figure of Speech

"nubile"
spat nastily
gorgeous girlhood lusted
for, unattainable, raises
old bile

Load Factor

airline

seats are like this

once missed, they're gone. Lost as

we separate
            unkissed
                        address

not kept

Fortress

There are four of you in this photograph,
digital, smiling, holding hands
two lads two whites two girls two blacks
and the fortress stands brick-stone around you.

One of you bought me a litre of rum.
That was yesterday in thanks:
because of me two were rescued from the reef
when rising surf had you floundering.

The women both know this, are grateful.
The men once knew this, but are already busy
forgetting
there was any deep obligation.

Which of course there is not.
I'm nosy. That's why I noticed your struggle
while others thought you yelled for fun or attention.
Though deaf, I could read your waves from that distance.

You're welcome. Of course you won't know this
with all contact lost, dropped like my business card
once you reached home and the incident shrank, walled off
behind better memories.

There must be other images of fortresses.
I have this one.

Excerpt

forgot

what's to live for

whoever decided?

nothing can change your mind that you

forget

Last Place Look

or
Grave Terns

no tern

complains unstoned

stern tones
            profane silence

grave birds proclaim
                no stone remains

unterned

Herd in Eulogy

heaven
without rain, heaven
without bodies hunger wanting, heaven
without choice or sin or loneliness, heaven
without hope or growth or fear just unrelenting
heaven
sounds like death

Rug Strains

rug,
what the hell is that
scattered along the floor?
something the cat just shagged on?
or just part of a puking throw
away comment?

it avoids being a hall runner
by staying in place, sort-of,
yet bunches up to spoil fast starts.

pet barf doesn't curl it,
but like all uses abuses,
effort pays to clean up misadventure.

the rug itself lacks sensation.

a bear rug, now that would be different.
I could stop a hall runner with one of those
quickly scattered to shag on
bunching up to accept fast starts.

what's common to fact and fantasy here:
hard floor under knees
and cleaning up after pussy.

Not Yet

like this
whispers each wave
caressing curves on shore
swim suit eyes hold wanting patience
maybe

Can't-or, or Don't Stagger the Horses

You
   ought
      not
   to
                     force
               intercourse
               on a horse
         it can't form intent
   and can't whisper consent
an "accept-ion" of course
 can occur when the horse
               lying spent on your bed
                  so content giving head
            is that mouth-off, Mister Ed

Post Script

In time

I'll write again

as if I felt something

that could have mattered to someone

some time

Dream Prelude

Three small words, so soft to face
I stand stiff: dare not embrace -
what to say? betray sweet trust?
Could I stay? admit my lust?
Do I mean, to top such grace?

In my mind: herself in lace,
then no clothes: my motives, base -
She breathes out: above her bust
three small words.

I should leave, in shaky pace:
Must not take, cannot replace,
in this world, her offer, just
too much gift. My worth is dust.
Yet may I, in dreams, retrace
three small words.

Last Request

louder
you must purr louder,
block out street noise; siren
in my soft pounding heart: please purr
louder

Top View

each roof

blonde, blurs silver

under rinsing fall rain:

seasons bleaching
              past life colours

grey-ward

Famous Couple

pas de deux

our romance with fame
choreographed by public handlers
we circled each other, practising
seductive close contact, sensuous
rhythmic approach for teasing withdrawal
until we each achieved our solo spotlights
playing one by one for teeming others,
the applause of lustful sighs,
dual circles of separate spectators
distinct
and apart on our final stage of darkness
closing scene

pas
    de deux

How Pets Masturbate

(I)

cats are
really picky
each lick must land just right
dogs perversely just need people
watching

(II)

gold fish
fluff their own fins;
bettas hump at mirrors;
tetras, all frustration, simply
quiver

Silence

silence

lets memory

sing about love and life:

spring winning summer, loss in fall,

winter

Complication

at last

consummated

where does *it* go from here?

we must redress to separate

houses

Dream Ending

I stared
not to be scared
at height as eagles soared
till down looked doubt: my stomach soured

coward

Mal-A-prop-os

diet?

blondes *look* hotter

slender, cool brunettes *want*
better figures? Figure better!

Dye it!

Slurred

bar stool
what does that mean
some turd drinking whiskey
Kid Loudest can't keep straight in his
high chair

Assumption

blondes have
more fun? do blondes
love fuck better? have blondes
just been funded more? do blondes have
more?   fun?

Stranger

too much
or just asleep
face on bar past closing
does he dream how he got left out
last time

Lost Word

cheated.

not "forever"
not even one lifetime.

that's what you get, believing in

romance

Ending II

last call
lone whippoorwill
curdles dusk autumn's sky:

how did our summer come to fall
  apart

Chorus

play it again, sam
love's lust refrain to make the dancers
sway
passing each to each an invisible breeze
breathing of want this watcher feels
like an exhalation
as each slim girl sighs out
to bow for applause, stretching down
wish granted

later
wind naked
you arch above me, gusting
while in my brain that chorus pulses with us
again, again sam stroke it again sam
finally you bow, touching down
as if for applause
breathless
wish granted

By Word Play

a trophy wife, once

like relationship, faded:

wince, atrophy, wife

Perf Action

tearable corners:

. . . .

daytimers lacking these rip

```
              -~-
~~__ - __ ---- __  /   __ ---~ ~
```

terrible corners

In Motley

cocked hat
what does it mean?
his brain's set to go off?
maybe his mouth isn't stable
either?

Bias

gay guys
run for queer cure
brag about "best cancer"
makes me so mad I really can't
see straight

Mary's Ram

Mary had a little, clown
pretended she was plastered;
tried to pull her panties down
she mumbled: no, no bastard

Mary, have some more champagne
she says, real agony
should you reach my crotch again
don't lay that gun on me

Mary, I am shooting blanks
since my vasectomy
Mary murmurs, goodness, thanks,
feels up for sex to me

The Feeder

trustless
such petty birds
won't come down till I'm gone
air miracles, like angels, high
in doubt

Something Fishy

rod stroke
keeps fly twitching
bait in the eyes of prey
soft splash cast enticing gaping
fish lips

In Equality

special
interest groups
piss me up tight. How dare
you claim more right than this one, my
selfish?

Prance Smarming

old fox

charm prancing, winks;

waylaid lithe lady leans

away from waning smile:
                    , no
                        , prince

, charming

Bait

sparrows

fuck off,
        repeat

copulating chorus

cheep, was it good for you
                        while hawks

hover

Slick Move

seagull
improbably
wing-spoons downward, tasting
incredible luck: this slick is
fishy

Revoir

dawn drifts
smear shovel marks
hard tracks disappear, night's
evidence lost: love promise you
vanish

Memorab-il-y-a

burrs, like
minded moments
on exit shoes, laced tongues,
things we zip-mouthed away from, snagged
fester

Shillelagh Memento

key chain
violent stick
gift Irish trinket, twists
like you, doors open: step outside
you're gone

Burqa Metaphor

camel

herded female

trudges wellward, faithful

 commodity.
            sand
                    veiled eyes
                            just

bearing

Last Disbeliefs

don't talk afterlife:
like Santa Clause, I've heard those
childish fantasies

Hell, Resurrection?
imagine my surprise if
either turns out true

Instinct

What must a tree think
to make it shed its leaves admitting
the rude advances of fall and winter
does it wish for a breathless ecstasy
in that shivering approach
to make it glad to drop such finery
seducing itself to what base fulfilment
of nakedness
as it does what it must do

and was it just some instinct
made you undress for me
when you dropped your sheer and lacey finery
were you anticipating
such ravishing and rushed advances
was this fulfilment what you wanted
to make my breath come ragged
in a clumsy ecstasy
as we do what we must do

I pace past midnight by the window wondering,
watching the tree stand the chilling of its season;
will you expect support for a new life, come springtime,
why do we writhe in a parody of pain
to exult in pleasure
we must be just the fools of our own genetic programs,
or is there some reality in wanting
the repeated predictable orgasm;
did you ever watch me sleeping,
thick as a log after words of love and snoring,
did it make you wonder
what does a tree feel,
under the bark of familiar limbs
is behaviour more than instinct moving
when veins begin to stir
or just a reflex reaching leaves and flesh

ReForms of Intelligence

Intelligent plants
would go insane, and speaking dogs
would bark off the issues then break to reconvene
around a fireplug;
gesturing sign language chimps would embarrass supporters
by upsetting the press with mad banana moves;
and although dolphins navigate and sing
for sure without property they can't support causes,
and lacking thumbs, don't make opposable motions;
even talking mynah birds that oddly make sense
are as likely to mimic a vote request
as to shout "yea" to it.
There's a reason only humans construct complex laws
through deep deliberation with complicated speeches:
it's because we can keep shifting ground
                    around things we're discussing,
which climaxes when shaping legislation:
debating dogs can't do it,
and intelligent plants would go insane.

Library March

left out
all March Break week
  nothing to do but read
no home for holiday, no friends
    to call

Leading Questions

I lead you follow
what do you see
do you look beyond my footprints in the forest
hearing the crunch of leaves the snap of a twig;
if we pause at the edge of a thicket to find a bluejay
do you hear its jeer like a confirmation;
reaching the bay of the beaver pond wet shiny turtles
sunning along a log
dive into circling ripples in an instant
what do you see

you lead I follow
what do you see
as I watch you search a path between swamp and granite
the hills and hollows of our outdoor beings
seeking the softest slope the quietest passage
slowing in shadowed approach before each clearing
to arrive unexpected
by the startling birds and turtles
turning to nod with a gesture asking for silence
what do you see

You lead I follow
returning to cabin chill while I stoke the woodfire
you are turning down bedsheets
pulling the early curtains switching the light
watching me watch you in your dresser mirror
what do you see
as you undo buttons letting the zipper slip
on your faded blue jeans
hearing my shoes unfasten a rush of shirtsleeves
pulling off clothes that are crumpled in an instant
of urgency
what do you see

I lead you follow
lovemaking seems so natural after the walk
moving two by two our steps legs intertwine
you who tread so softly breathe like a coming windstorm
caught
in my hair like the bending branches twigs of a tree
what do you see
as I feel your navigation of hills and hollow
I remember the ruffed grouse mating call giant fingers
wings drumming along a leg
in our dusky darkness reaching breath's final quickness
what do you see

Lyrics: Madonna

I hate the sin, and love the sinner;
love the song, and hate the singer.

Blonde sex yourself
gender bender
like a prayer, you move over me in dreams
if Einstein can't play at dice with the world
you should not gamble with aids and lovers
baby
unlikely rumours
so many *friends* but no volunteer fathers
La isla bonita   could a boy   love this girl

such sexy music
such lustful lyrics
how many of us dream
of a night with you kept awake in torment
till morning riding
mounted sidesaddle any position at all
might become unstable in the real light of day
would friends in our own world mock on our return
did you make the beast of two backs with her
or two sides or whatever positional power
did occur to Her imagined
self
interest

in the dark I turn my earphones up and listen
I love the song and hate the singer;
lust for the singer, and hear your song.

Food by the Window

(Cinquain 101)

nuthatch
lands on the ledge
but he does not trust me
crouched as a cat behind the screen
watching

On Booting the Old Machine

On the corner of the basement table, the old machine is booting
- needs a poweron password -
so pull the keyboard out where I can reach it
and set the mousepad down here too
turn the screen around a bit more that's OK

and there it is, finally,
with the Icons that took me hours to get so nice,
square letters and colours
in the folders of tools and documents; let's begin.

since it's getting flaky,
set up an interface to send critical files
across to the Big Machine
then have a last look around in this old clunker
for some forgotten toy that might be fun.

Notice how slowly the screen refreshes,
and how tacky this ball mouse feels.
What a drag,
this used to be the fastest machine in the house.

It feels like looking back at a home once lived in
down a street we played along with hide and seek.
We expect to meet old friends but don't recognize them.
It seems odd that this place felt natural,
and that every small move opened a fresh adventure.

If I had to go back now I'd not stay long.
My habits have grown too close to my present furniture.
All the games seem awkward, ancient animation
looks a waste of time once the cards are finally dealt.

Funny, though, when the old screen does go dark,
how we feel for a second the loss that it was then
when we had to stop for supper or time to sleep.
That's one thing that progress never changes,
our regret at seeing a part of ourselves shut down.

Opossum Memories

possum
memories play
dead in our brains, words hide
lying down under synonyms
for "lost"

A Question of Taste

orange
butterflies mate
on earth which cattle hooves
have cut to mud, strange place to choose
for sex

Two Silent Speeches

  I feel
death reach for you
watching your bravery
hiding pain, fear, is just too much
to bear

life was
a pleasure, you
always made so much fun
thanks for visiting, do go on
  after

From Fixed Positions

tiresome	pleasant,
work ache of arms	work ache of arms
soft luxury, stiff back	missed luxury, stiff back
resented pushing numb on this	remembered riding numb on this
wheeled chair	wheeled chair

For Professionals Only

or, Not Exactly as Shown

Do not try these movements at home, these are professional athletes!
Do not expect these bargains locally, these are professional shop-letes!
Do not attempt these expressions with friends, these are professional
smirk-letes!
Do not mind these concepts yourself, these are professional thought-
letes!
Do not test these arguments anywhere, these are professional
politicians!
Do not trust these claims at all, this is professional marketing!

Just Add Bureaucracy, or

How a Cinquain Shrinks to a Haiku

rock breaks
scissors, scissors
cut paper, while paper
covers rock. add bureaucracy
and get

rock sharpens scissors
scissors challenge red tape, but
red tape smothers rock

Flight Dreams

shadows
of hummingbirds
asleep on wallpaper
move through my daughter's dreams of flight
all night

Sleep Gets Deeper

Sleep gets deeper
with age and exhaustion
as an act of escape
to abandon consciousness
in gentle dark withdrawal comforted
we can rest as if forever with the light out
lying still in any position
without snoring or at least dozing through it
in the strange dreams that come to an afternoon nap
as if our spirits questioned death, and were answered
in the strange dreams that come to an afternoon nap
without snoring or at least dozing through it
lying still in any position
we can rest as if forever with the light out
in gentle dark withdrawal comforted
to abandon consciousness
as an act of escape
with age and exhaustion
sleep gets deeper

On the Spider Screen

When we have all sequenced genomes
plus perfectly understood embryogenesis
with total comprehension of every protein
and its folding and charges plus the timing
of it's gene's expression
pattern across all tissues and cells
will we understand everything

meanwhile the night time spider
weaves its patterned web outside my cabin window
measuring its spiral funnel against the squares
of my flyscreen grid of civilization;

does it know of other genomes out there driven
on wings of turbulent lift parameters
toward it in fatal phototropism

and the silver moth of amber-jewelled eyes
knows nothing of electric light or flyscreen
or the cosmos that brings about hours of moonless darkness
nor elastic limit strength of sticky threads;
it does not comprehend its web of death
nor its complexity in the eyes that watch it
on the spider screen

(A Meaty Speech)

Quoth Steer:
 we are not cowed
  nor macho bull stuff us;
   even in death we are the beef
patties

Leaving

guard rail
ripples away
bus windows streak distance
god keep looking scrub these glasses
no tears

Fortress of Solitude

brown plastic chair
under the bare pear tree
and in shade of a green tin shed
almost not visible
from the bird feeder:
squirrels and pigeons underneath
face one brown hopping cardinal
till enough house sparrows to choke a large cat
flutter and disturb each other
to settle down again;
if the wind moves empty branches
and gently stirs brown downed oak leaves
while sifting
through fruitless raspberry canes
without any whispering

it means nobody's coming
or going